W9-BSU-039

FAR-OUT and UNUSUAL pets

Hissing Cockroaches

Cool Pets!

Alvin and Virginia Silverstein
and Laura Silverstein Nunn

Enslow Elementary
an imprint of
Enslow Publishers, Inc.

40 Industrial Road
Box 398
Berkeley Heights, NJ 07922
USA

http://www.enslow.com

Enslow Elementary, an imprint of Enslow Publishers, Inc.

Enslow Elementary® is a registered trademark of Enslow Publishers, Inc.

Library of Congress Cataloging-in-Publication Data
Silverstein, Alvin.
 Hissing cockroaches : cool pets! / by Alvin and Virginia Silverstein, and Laura Silverstein Nunn.
   p. cm. — (Far-out and unusual pets series)
 Includes bibliographical references and index.
 ISBN 978-0-7660-3685-7
 1. Madagascar hissing cockroach—Juvenile literature. 2. Cockroaches as pets—Juvenile literature.
I. Silverstein, Virginia B. II. Nunn, Laura Silverstein. III. Title.
 QL505.7.B4S55 2011
 595.7'28—dc22
                            2010020884

Printed in the United States of America

102010 Lake Book Manufacturing, Inc., Melrose Park, IL

10 9 8 7 6 5 4 3 2 1

To Our Readers: We have done our best to make sure all Internet Addresses in this book were active and appropriate when we went to press. However, the author and the publisher have no control over and assume no liability for the material available on those Internet sites or on other Web sites they may link to. Any comments or suggestions can be sent by e-mail to comments@enslow.com or to the address on the back cover.

Enslow Publishers, Inc., is committed to printing our books on recycled paper. The paper in every book contains 10% to 30% post-consumer waste (PCW). The cover board on the outside of each book contains 100% PCW. Our goal is to do our part to help young people and the environment too!

Photo Credits: Alamy: © Alessandro Mancini, p. 7, © Frances Roberts, p. 36; © Dick Michael/ Animals Animals - Earth Scenes, p. 12; © iStockphoto.com/David Coder, p. 13; Jasper Nance, p. 16 (bottom); © Dr. Jay A. Yoder and Dr. Joshua B. Benoit, p. 30; © Jonathan Donovan, p. 23; OSF/Photolibrary, p. 25; © Pete Oxford/Minden Pictures, p. 4; © Phil Myers, Animal Diversity Web, p. 20; © Robert & Linda Mitchell, pp. 42, 44; Shutterstock.com, pp. 1, 3, 16 (top), 19, 33, 38; © Sky Bonillo/PhotoEdit, p. 10; © Tom McHugh/Photo Researchers, Inc., p. 15.

Illustration Credits: © 2010 Gerald Kelley, www.geraldkelley.com

Cover Photo: Shutterstock.com

Contents

Hissing cockroaches make cool and unusual pets.

Giant Cockroach!

Just thinking about cockroaches makes most people want to scream: "Eew! Gross!" They picture cockroaches scurrying across their kitchen floor. They watch in horror as hundreds of them swarm along the walls looking for a place to hide in the cracks.

Not all people think cockroaches are creepy, though. In fact, some people actually keep cockroaches as pets. The most popular cockroach pet is the hissing cockroach. These cockroaches are not the same as those annoying pests that sneak around people's homes at night. Hissing cockroaches actually make good pets. They are also a popular animal in museums, zoos, and classrooms.

Are Cockroaches Dirty?

Many people think of cockroaches as dirty. But pet hissing cockroaches are actually clean animals.

Cockroach pests are a different story. They can carry germs. They often travel through sewers and other unclean places. Then they come into people's homes and crawl on their food!

What makes the hissing cockroach so special? This cockroach is famous for the hissing noise it makes. That's how it got its name. If it gets upset or annoyed, it will hiss, sort of like a snake. It is rather surprising when you hear it. Luckily, hissing cockroaches don't bite—unlike a hissing snake!

Hissing cockroaches can grow to be about three inches (ten centimeters) long!

The hissing cockroach is one of the world's biggest cockroaches. It may grow up to three inches (ten centimeters) long. For a cockroach, that's big! It's three times the length of an average household cockroach.

After All These Years . . .

Cockroaches have been around for more than 300 million years! That's long before the dinosaurs roamed the earth. After all these years, cockroaches today look about the same as they did back then. They have hardly changed at all. That's why people sometimes call them "living fossils."

The more you learn about the hissing cockroach, the more you'll realize that this is no ordinary bug. Read on to find out what makes the hissing cockroach such a far-out and unusual pet.

2

A Cockroach for a Pet?

People keep all kinds of unusual pets—potbellied pigs, mice, rats, lizards, snakes, and even ants. So why not cockroaches? A hissing cockroach can be just as cool as any other unusual pet. Many people don't realize this because they think that *all* cockroaches are dirty and gross. Actually, though, hissing cockroaches are gentle, harmless creatures.

What do you know about hissing cockroaches? Before you decide to buy one, it's a good idea to find out a bit about its natural way of living. The way these animals act in the wild will give you an idea of what to expect when keeping one as a pet.

Having a hissing cockroach as a pet can be a great experience.

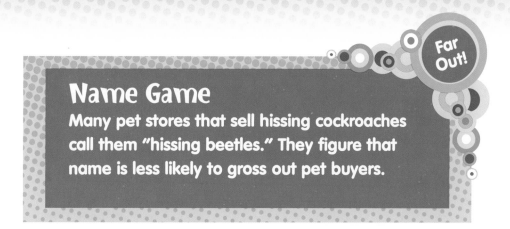

Name Game

Many pet stores that sell hissing cockroaches call them "hissing beetles." They figure that name is less likely to gross out pet buyers.

Where Do Hissing Cockroaches Live?

Cockroaches usually live in warm, damp places. Hissing cockroaches are found in Madagascar, an island off the east coast of Africa. They are commonly called Madagascar hissing cockroaches. During the day, they hide in rotting logs and fallen leaves on the forest floor. At night, they come out to look for food. They eat fallen fruit and leaves, as well as rotting animals and plants.

Hissing cockroaches live in very large groups, called colonies. A large colony may number in the hundreds! Within the colony there are a number of family groups. Each family includes one male cockroach, several females, and their children.

In the wild, hissing cockroaches live on the forest floors of Madagascar.

The place where the cockroaches eat, sleep, and breed is called their territory. The male is in charge of defending his family's territory. He will fight any other males that try to come into his territory.

Females, on the other hand, can come and go without any trouble.

As pets, these cockroaches still keep their wild ways. So if you want a colony of cockroaches, make sure there is just one male. Otherwise, you might see a hissing fight take place.

About one hundred hissing cockroaches can live together in a colony.

Hissy Fits!

How do you know when a hissing cockroach gets upset? It hisses! It may hiss for other reasons, as well. For example, two males may hiss when they battle over territory. Males may also hiss when they want to attract females.

How do hissing cockroaches make hissing sounds? A cockroach breathes through a row of tiny holes along each side of its body. When a hissing cockroach blows air out of these holes quickly, it makes a hissing sound.

Far Out!

The Hissing Cockroach Up Close

The hissing cockroach is an insect. Like any insect, it has six legs. It also has three body parts: the head, the thorax, and the abdomen.

The head is the smallest part, but it is very important. The two eyes at the front are very good

If you have more than one hissing cockroach, watch them carefully to see if they get along.

Hissing cockroaches have three main body parts: head, thorax, and abdomen.

Hissing cockroaches have compound eyes, which are made up of thousands of individual lenses. This helps hissing cockroaches spot moving objects, but they are not able to focus on objects the way we do.

at spotting moving things, such as other insects. The cockroach's mouth has moving parts for biting and chewing food. Two long antennae on the head act as "feelers." They are covered with tiny hairs that are very sensitive to touch. The antennae can move around to feel where things are. They can also be used to smell things. A male cockroach uses his antennae to find a female cockroach by her smell.

The thorax is the middle body part of the cockroach. Its six legs are attached to the thorax.

The abdomen is the largest body part. It is made up of ringlike segments (parts). They make this bug look a bit like an armadillo.

Hissing cockroaches can't fly. Unlike most cockroaches, they don't have wings.

Insects don't have bones. They have a hard outer covering called an exoskeleton. The word exoskeleton means "skeleton on the outside." A cockroach's exoskeleton covers its entire body. The covering acts like a suit of armor. It protects

Can a Cockroach Actually Live Without a Head?

Scientists have found that a cockroach can live for a few *weeks* without its head! If a cockroach somehow loses its head, the neck can seal itself off. That way it doesn't bleed to death.

How can a cockroach live without a brain? It has nerves in each body segment. They allow it to do simple things, such as stand, react to touch, and move around. So the cockroach can actually move around even though its head is missing!

Without a head, though, the cockroach can't eat. Eventually, it will die.

Far Out!

The abdomen is made of ringlike segments.

Hissing cockroaches are good climbers.

the cockroach's soft insides. It also helps to hold water inside its body.

Cockroaches are excellent climbers. Each foot has two claws on the end. The feet and front legs also have sticky pads and hooks. They help the cockroach walk on smooth, slippery surfaces, such as glass windows.

Most cockroaches can run really fast. (If you've ever seen one scurry across the kitchen floor, you know what we mean!) But hissing cockroaches are slow movers. That's good news if you own one. You don't want to have to chase it all over the house!

3

A Home for Your Cockroach

Normally, people try to keep cockroaches *out* of their homes. But the hissing cockroach is special. This isn't the kind of insect you'd want to squash. You'll want to keep it alive and healthy. That means keeping it warm, cozy, and fed. Although hissing cockroaches are tough insects, they do best when living conditions are close to those in the wild.

Make your hissing cockroach's home similar to its
natural home in the wild.

You don't have to go to Madagascar, though, to get a hissing cockroach. Many pet stores sell them. You can also get them from breeders—people who raise hissing cockroaches.

How Many Pet Cockroaches?

How many hissing cockroaches should you get? Should you get just one? Remember, cockroaches in the wild live in groups (colonies). So getting more than one is a good idea. It will help your cockroach pets feel more at home.

Is it better to get only males or females or both? And how can you tell the difference? When they are fully grown, it is very easy to tell a male

Far Out!

A Long Life?

Hissing cockroaches live from two to five years. That's longer than most insects. Some insects do not live for more than a year. Others last only months or even weeks. And some live just for a few days.

Both males and females have horns, but the male's are larger.

from a female. An adult male hissing cockroach has two "horns" on its head. A female has horns, too. But they are much smaller. The male's antennae are also bigger and more feathery than the female's.

Get Ready to Rumble!

When two male cockroaches come face to face, they will get ready for a battle to see who's boss. At first, they go after each other using their antennae in a kind of sword fight. Then the males hiss fiercely. Next, they rush each other. Like two rams going head to head, they butt each other with their horns. They keep crashing into each other until one finally backs off. The winner gets his choice of females.

Far Out!

If you don't want your cockroaches to breed, then you want all females. A male and a female will breed if you keep them together. And if you get more than one male, the males will probably fight. It doesn't matter that they are not living in the wild. They will consider their new home their territory. It will be in their nature to battle.

All the Comforts of Home

A 10- to 15-gallon tank is a good size to keep several hissing cockroaches. But if you plan on keeping more, you will need a 20-gallon tank or larger. The tank should have a tightly fitted mesh covering.

Cockroaches are excellent climbers. With sticky pads and hooks on their legs and feet, they can easily climb the glass walls of the tank. They are also very sneaky. They can slip out of the tank without your even realizing it. To keep your cockroaches from escaping, try this little trick: Smear some petroleum jelly around the entire

inside of the tank, a few inches below the top.
The cockroaches won't be able to climb past this
slippery surface. Put on new petroleum jelly as
needed, to keep your pets from escaping.

Cover the bottom of the tank with wood chips or tree bark. Make sure there are some hiding places. These can be pieces of cardboard egg cartons or toilet paper rolls spread throughout. Your pets should also have branches for climbing.

Keep the tank in a warm place. Remember, hissing cockroaches are from Madagascar. Madagascar is a tropical place. It is usually warm there all year round. But it is also rather damp.

Far Out!

Turn Up the Heat

Turn up the heat, and a pair of hissing cockroaches will turn into baby-making machines. At high temperatures, these insects breed quickly. In fact, temperatures in the upper 80s°F (about 30°C) and higher are perfect conditions for breeding. (If the temperature gets below the mid-70s F, or about 24°C, they will not breed at all.) Hissing cockroaches breed so easily that there are plenty of new ones for pet stores to sell. In fact, there is no need to take hissing cockroaches from the wild anymore.

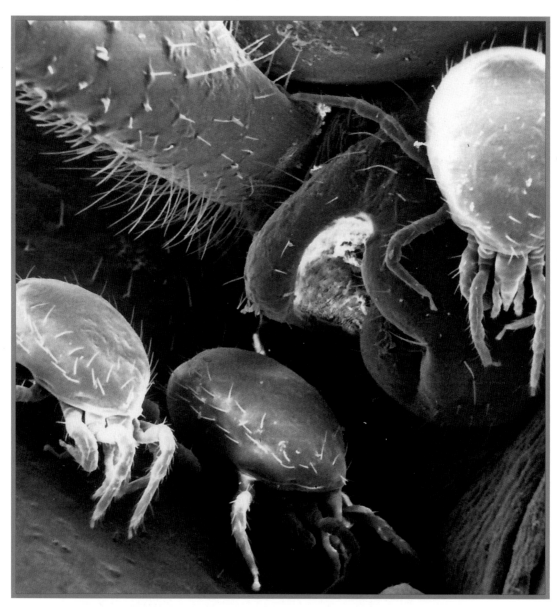

Check your pet cockroach to make sure it is not crawling with tiny mites. (These mites are magnified many times larger than they are in real life.)

My Cockroach Has Bugs!

Don't be surprised if you find little bugs crawling on your cockroach. Just as dogs can get fleas, hissing cockroaches sometimes carry tiny spider-like creatures called mites. These mites do not live on other animals or people—only on the cockroaches. This can happen if the tank gets dirty. (It should be cleaned at least once a month.)

How do you get rid of these mites? Put your cockroach in a plastic bag containing a small amount of flour. Then gently shake the plastic bag. The mites should fall off the cockroach and into the flour. Remove the cockroach, tie up the bag, and throw it in the trash. Gently spray the cockroach with water to remove the extra flour. The mites may also be removed by brushing the cockroach with a small paintbrush.

Keep your cockroach out of direct sunlight. Otherwise it might dry out. It is a good idea to spray water in the tank every day or two.

Hissing cockroaches do well in temperatures that are at least 75°F (24°C). When it is warmer, they will be more active. You may need to use a heating pad underneath the tank. That will help keep the cockroaches warm and comfortable.

What Do Cockroaches Eat?

In the wild, hissing cockroaches eat whatever is around. This may be anything from fallen fruit and leaves to rotting animal and plant life. And so, your cockroach pets will eat just about anything you give them. You can feed them dry dog, cat, or mouse food. You should also give them fruits and vegetables cut up into small pieces. Some popular choices are orange slices, banana peels, carrots, apples, grapes, squash, peas, and potato slices.

Fruits and vegetables give the cockroaches much of the water they need. However, you should also

Feed your hissing cockroach fruits and vegetables.

give them a shallow dish of drinking water with cotton balls on the bottom. The cotton soaks up the water, and the cockroaches suck the water up from the cotton. (They might drown if you put just water in the dish.) Be sure to replace the old food every other day, before it starts smelling bad. You should replace the cotton ball and water, as well.

4

Living With Your Pet Cockroach

What can you do with a hissing cockroach pet? It's not the same as keeping an ant colony. You can only *watch* ants. You can't take them out and play with them. If you did, you'd end up with ants loose in the house. And you'd probably never *see* them again. (Your parents wouldn't be too happy, either!) But one of the fun things about owning a hissing cockroach is that you *can* take it out and play with it. Luckily, this insect moves slowly enough that you *can* catch it.

Play with your pet
cockroach!

Night-Night

If you keep the cockroach tank in your bedroom, you may get woken up. Hissing cockroaches are most active at night. They'll rustle around digging, climbing, and eating. And if you are keeping a colony with more than one male, the males may get a bit rowdy.

Handling Your Pet Cockroach

Want to freak out your friends? Just have a couple of hissing cockroaches crawl up and down your arms. That'll do the trick! It may look kind of creepy to them, but it's actually pretty cool.

Hissing cockroaches aren't as scary as they look. They aren't poisonous. They don't bite. And they don't smell bad. But don't be surprised if your cockroach hisses when you first try to pick it up. Don't take it personally. It hisses because it's nervous. It just doesn't know you yet.

Generally, cockroaches don't like being touched. In fact, just touch its back and you'll hear it hiss.

Let your pet cockroach get used to being picked up.

Still, it's a good idea to handle your cockroach often. Eventually, it will get used to you. It will know you by smell.

A hissing cockroach may be a little prickly to hold for the first time. Besides the claws on its feet, its legs are covered with sharp little spines.

They can grab onto your skin. If you try to jerk the insect off you, ouch! Be careful or you might hurt the cockroach, too. So always be gentle.

With one hand, pick the cockroach up by the thorax. (Remember, that's the middle part, right behind its head.) Then place it on the flat palm of your other hand. Let the cockroach crawl from one hand to the other. Or let it travel up your arms. Carefully pick it up, place it back on your palm, and do it all over again.

Baby Boom

Breeding hissing cockroaches can be a lot of fun. But watch out! A small colony of just a few cockroaches can quickly become a really big colony. A female can have twenty to forty babies at one time!

Most insects lay eggs. But you won't see a hissing cockroach lay eggs. Babies hatch from eggs while they are still inside the mother's body. The mother gives birth to live young, called nymphs.

Too Many Cockroaches

Cockroaches breed so quickly that you can end up with more than one hundred before you know it. Then the tank will be way too crowded. Colonies should not be too large.

What can you do with the babies? Actually, you should figure this out *before* you start breeding your cockroaches. You will need to find them a new home. Perhaps your friends will take some. Or you can give them to a zoo. Maybe your school will be willing to take some as class pets.

What if there is no other place they can go? Then you probably should not keep males and females together. Or keep the temperature of their cage cool enough so they don't breed. You don't want to let hissing cockroaches loose in the neighborhood. Remember, they come from a very different part of the world. They could have unexpected effects on the plants and animals living in your area.

Baby hissing cockroaches are called nymphs.

A nymph looks like a tiny adult hissing cockroach.
It is about a quarter inch long. That's about the
size of a small watermelon seed. And it is very flat.
The nymphs may stick close to the mother for
awhile after they come out. The mother protects
them by keeping her body over them.

Growing Up

The nymphs grow very quickly. As the little cockroach grows, though, its exoskeleton gets very tight. (Remember, it's like hard armor, not a soft, stretchy covering like your skin.) The young cockroach has to shed its exoskeleton to get more room to grow. This is called molting. When a cockroach is ready to molt, it usually goes off to be alone. So if you see a "loner," keep an eye on it. You might be in for a show.

When a cockroach starts to molt, it first puffs up its body full of air. This causes a seam, or weak spot, in the exoskeleton to pop open. Once the seam breaks open, the cockroach forces out all the air it has taken in. It starts wriggling around inside its too-tight exoskeleton. Finally, it breaks free. Underneath is the new covering. It is pure white and very soft. (It's not a good idea to handle a cockroach while it is molting. You might hurt it.) Once it's out, the cockroach draws in more air to

When a hissing cockroach molts, it breaks out of its exoskeleton and finds a safe place to hide until its new covering becomes hard.

puff up its body to its new full size. As the new exoskeleton hardens, it gets darker.

A nymph will go through six molts until it reaches adult size. This may take five to ten months. By then it will be more than twelve times as big as when it was born.

* * *

Some people say that hissing cockroaches make perfect pets. They won't hurt you. They don't take up much room. They are fun to watch, especially in a colony. You get to see how they work together to build their colony. You can also see how they get along—or don't. And best of all, you can see it all right in your own house.

Words to Know

abdomen—The rear body part of an insect, located behind the thorax.

antennae—A pair of long, thin body parts on the head of some animals, including insects. They sense touch and smell.

breed—To mate animals and raise their young.

colony—A group of animals or plants of the same kind living together.

exoskeleton—The hard outer shell or covering of many animals, especially insects.

molt—To shed hair, skin, or feathers.

nymph—The young form of some insects.

segment—One of several parts or pieces that fit with others to make up a whole object.

territory—The area where an animal lives and gets its food.

thorax—The middle body part of an insect, located between the head and the abdomen.

Learn More

Books

Birch, Robin. *Cockroaches Up Close*. Chicago: Raintree, 2005.

Harrington, Jane. *Extreme Pets!* New York: Scholastic, Inc., 2007.

Kalman, Bonnie, and Rebecca Sjonger. *Everyday Insects*. New York: St. Catharines, Ont.: Crabtree Pub., 2006.

Web Sites

Discovery Kids.
http://yucky.discovery.com/flash/roaches

Los Angeles Zoo and Botanical Gardens: Madagascar Hissing Cockroach.
http://www.lazoo.org/animals/invertebrates/madagascarhissingcockroach/

Madagascar Giant Hissing Cockroaches.
http://aqualandpetsplus.com/Bug,%20Madagascar%20Hissing%20Roach.htm

Index